Talkers Through Dream Doors

D1324099

c r o c u s

Talkers Through Dream Doors

Poetry and Short Stories
by Black Women

First published in 1989 by Crocus

Crocus books are published by
Commonword Ltd,
Cheetwood House,
21 Newton Street,
Manchester M1 1FZ.

Commonword gratefully acknowledges financial assistance from the
Association of Greater Manchester Authorities, North West Arts
Association and Manchester City Council.

Typeset and printed by Rap Ltd, Rochdale, OL12 7AF.

British Library Cataloguing in Publication Data

Talkers through dream doors: poetry and short stories by black women
writers.
    1. English literature. Black women writers, 1945 —.
    Anthologies
    820.8'09287

ISBN 0 946745 60 9

CONTENTS

Foreword

When I was sent this collection, it was with hope that
I would enjoy it. Having read the poems and short
stories, I am still not sure that 'enjoy' is the most
appropriate word. I read with a mixture of pain, anger,
laughter, joy and pride.

When I was a child, growing up in Britain, my
literary diet consisted mainly of stories which told of
would be prima ballerinas or Grand National winners,
but as a Black working class family, ballet classes or
horse riding lessons weren't part of our experience.
It was like reading about an alien world. There weren't
many books like this so, I often felt very much alone.
I used to scribble onto paper my own thoughts and
dreams. Of course time, or a self-protecting
mechanism, has blurred the memory, but this book
eased open the floodgates. One of the earliest poems
that I do remember was a catalogue of the racist abuse
I'd experienced as a teenager: employers telling me that
'the vacancy has just been filled' or other children
shouting 'Nigger, go home'. The poem ended '...and
the man from God said 'My Child' and opened his
arms.'

Saturday evenings, sitting in the kitchen. The smell
of the paraffin heater, hot metal and burning hair. I
used to hold my ears, but still worried about the
possibility of having my fingers burned. Punishment?
Yes and no. My mother was pressing my hair with a

hot comb. Are there many Black women who don't remember the nervous shudder as the comb neared the hairline or the back of the neck? Read 'Simmy'. Then came the Afro. Freedom? Some of us who didn't have 'good' hair, suffered through the Afro Blow-Out kits. Then came the relaxers, when we'd pretend that the chemicals weren't burning the scalp yet, just so that we could be sure that our hair would be straight. And for what? Read 'Bad Hair'.

Many of the writings are about more than physical pain. Of course, there's the agony of being a battered wife or being sexually abused, but out of these pages comes the mental pain of being a Black woman in a white dominated, male-orientated society. How many times do we open a newspaper and weep inside when we read about yet another woman who has become the victim of violence? But what also emerges from these pages is the will to fight against helplessness:

> *We're not playthings, we are women*
> *not just here to be raped or mugged*
> *just because we feel like dancing*
> *and we go out all alone*
> *It doesn't mean we're looking for a man to*
> > *take us home...*
> *we are women...and we're human*
> *not just here for men to have.*

At the opposite extreme to 'Innocent Victim' is the hurt expressed in 'Home Truths'. I often wonder why, when I've spent most of my life in this society, I can still be shocked and pained by a simple act of thoughtlessness or deliberate snubs. I should have become accustomed to it, or hardened by it, but I still feel anger. Perhaps the anger is cathartic. Perhaps it makes a transition to the determination expressed in 'Raising of Lazarus' and many of the other poems.

When my mother came to this country in the fifties, a stranger with few friends, but with a young child, she worked hard to create a life for me. I still feel, as in 'Past and Present', that I would never have been able to cope as she did. But that's where our strength lies, in our mothers, sisters, aunts, nieces, daughters, grandmothers and great grandmothers. And that's why this book is important. It reconfirms my belief that across geographical and generational boundaries, we still *share*. With Black women writing and publishing books like this, other young Black women might never have to feel quite so alone.

Vastiana Belfon
Presenter, BBC's *Ebony*

Preface

These poems and stories have a special quality because they are focused through the lens of being female and Black. This perspective is expressed in the wistful sharing of 'Coffee Morning at Your House', the pride of 'Ebony Baby Girl' and the sense of injustice in 'Entertain Me With Love Stories'. In this poem, the conflict is communicated in the writer's desire to run away and the impossibility of escape:

Cries of my brother
Shatter the air
And the stillness and blue
Of the summer's destroyed
By the tears and despair...

It's immoral to have them strewn
Across my TV screen
Entice me with tempting products to buy
Entertain me with love stories, and comedy

even

But don't make my heart
Scream in silence
At my shame for living a fortunate life
Away from apartheid.

Even when these aspects of our lives are not in our conscious reactions, they qualify our submerged responses and, of course, they qualify, or even define, the way others see us. This is cleverly illustrated by the wry humour of 'The Right Mix':

We must have the right mix, she said
With a twinkle in her eye.
3 Whites, 1.5 West Indians and 1.4 Asians.
That's what our requirements are
To make our Project viable
And to give it credibility.

In this collection, personal observations about life also speak about the universals of human experience — death, love, alienation. Few poems express the despair of loneliness as powerfully as 'The Big Chair':

Had she spoken,
she might have said:
'Pretend that I'm asleep — I'm that far away!
You only dream you see me
staked through the heart
in the big chair.'

Thus, these pieces of writing demonstrate in various ways essential aspects of artistic creation — calling our attention to our shared humanity, drawing new images from careful observation and crafting words skilfully to persuade us into the writer's world view.

Difficult judgements had to be made as the panel struggled to make its choices. We argued the strengths and weaknesses of each piece of writing submitted. We wanted to be sure that each chosen piece had something new to say about the old archetypal themes. As we discussed the poems and stories, we had a powerful sense of developing writers whose work is still in process. This is what makes the collection exciting — the sense of the distance covered to reach the points represented by these words fixed on the page, and the promise of exciting destinations waiting for each of these writers.

I enjoyed working with the other members of the editing panel, most of whom are creative artists in their own right. We have been moved, amused and made to think, in the course of selecting the poems and stories presented here. British Black writing has been a postscript for too long. The writers in this anthology are in the process of making their statements in the main text.

Judy Craven
Afro-Caribbean Language Unit, Manchester

Introduction

Cultureword is a part of Commonword, publishers of Crocus books. Cultureword's role is to promote, support and encourage Afro-Caribbean and Asian writers of the North West. Its recent activities have included the publication of *Black and Priceless*, the first anthology from Asian and Afro-Caribbean writers in the North West, and the organisation of a Black writers competition, the winners of which were included in the book. Since Cultureword's inception three years ago the profile of the Black writer in education, the media, the arts and most importantly in his or her own community has risen.

Throughout the many and varied projects that Cultureword has initiated the profile of Black women writers has always been high. Hence the publication of 'Sistahs' magazine by Crocus books, the organisation of a Black women writers course by Commonword and Cultureword, the creation of a full time post to support and encourage Asian and Afro-Caribbean women writers and the subsequent development of regular Black women writers' workshops.

Talkers Through Dream Doors, includes poets, short story writers, novelists, playwrights, journalists and story-tellers, and is a testament not only to the power of Black women's literature, but to the wealth of talent coming from the Black women of our communities. The editing panel which consisted of Black women writers and educationalists, spent many enjoyable, and sometimes frustrating, hours in the process of selecting the work for this book. Sincere thanks go to Kanta Walker, Judy Craven, Nayaba Aghedo, Qaisra Shahraz and Louise Ansari.

A gross misunderstanding in England is that performance is second to the written craft — however historically the *first* poets were performance poets. Whilst many Black writers have achieved a high profile on the national writing scene through performance, this has lead to the creation of a stereotype of what Black writing is about. Is performance all that we do? After reading this anthology the celebrated writer Amrit Wilson answers: 'These are voices of a new generation of writers — powerful, sophisticated, sometimes startling. They reassert the Black identity and cross new boundaries to define it.'

Lemn Sissay
Cultureword — Asian and Afro-Caribbean writers development worker.

POETRY

CINDY ARTISTE

Dreams With Teeth
(For Evelyn)

The head on the desk
lets close a teary eye
which can't weep
because her dreams cry
'Not yet! Not yet!'

So with a sigh she
pushes her heavy head upright,
reaches again for the book,
adjusts the light,
flicks the pages 'til they snap
at her fingers like the beaks
of fledgling dreams.

She turns a page and turns it back,
re-reads it two? three? times,
gives her hair an angry yank,
moans, but makes no move away
from dreams with teeth.

By the door stand I —
the undiscovered witness —
fearing to tread
on the floor between us
where aborted beginnings lie
creased and peaceful in paper parcels.

Question: do I let sleeping dreams lie?
Or take heed to the pyramid of wasted paper
which slowly
rumples towards me
rustling complaints.

But, God! what is the password?
If only I knew it!

Or even this swollen shadow
who pins a pointed dream
to her throat and hugs it there
like a queen.

The stiffening shoulders
know I'm there.
I retreat silently,
leaving this straightbacked
stranger
hugging herself
and perched to fall neatly
down the sharp edge
of a dream.

The Big Chair

Though his caring feet left no sound
on the stairs,
the drum-beat at her temple
knows he's there.
The door creaks open
with what seems a sniper's precision
And it's the sound of her name
the bullet reports.
Is he literally 'nosing' her out?
Or is that her own sniffling she hears
as he nears
and finds her,
huddled in the big chair.

He doesn't even ask.
   Simply sits quietly for a while
and then quietly leaves.

She knows he lies awake upstairs
hoping it will pass sooner
rather than later —
or, at least, surface enough
so that she can need him.

He luxuriates in that need
while she
adds regret
to everything else that keeps her
in the big chair
in the dark.

Once he ventured:
'If you love me, like you say,
surely I can help?'

She couldn't even answer,
could only howl inside
in hopeful harmony
with the pain she was causing him.

Had she spoken:
she might have said
'Pretend I'm asleep — I'm that far away!
You only dream you see me
staked through the heart
in the big chair.'

Rescued From The Fire

I drink to misfits.
To spores
incubated too soon or too late.

I drink to mistakes.

I drink to the unwanted
who know it,
and wish them well
on their journey through Hell.

I drink.

I drink to the shepherds
without sheep,
to the divers of the Deep,
to the song-and-dance man
who can't carry a tune
in a can.

And then I dream.

I dream to misfits:
to the woman who, facing
a dish-filled sink,
claws into the nether cupboards
for a drink.
I dream to and for those
for whom it hurts to think.

I dream to mistakes,
to out-takes,
to the losing stakes.

The poor ye have with you always
and always.
But are You there?
Are You there?
Not knowing, I drink

to the disparity
of photos
showing glowing-skinned me
with a face as open and simple
as a Modigliani —
Don't laugh, I crack easily.

I dream
I drink
I discover
misfits — under the bed, usually,
or in the kitchen at 3
scurrying before I can cry
'Halt! It's me!'

On white nights
full of paranoia,
they stand, fixed,
in corners of the garden.
I break the water glass
to subtract a little from their burden,
and toss it out to them
to eat or wear
or slash their wrists
or what have you.

This —
you must take this as —
my testimony:
misfits tend not to thrive.

But if you rescue this
from the fire
Salut!
I drink to you.

Chesapeake Bay

She guessed it was a narrow escape.
She knew she shouldn't have laughed.
But she was fifteen.
Which was why she'd
beckoned her friends round the phone
to giggle at the pleading 'older man'
From a movie, she chose the phrase:
'My affection is beyond recall.'
And laughed, enjoying the role of femme fatale.

No entourage to impress,
she blushed next day to find him
waiting patiently on her route.
He suggested a walk.
Flustered, she shrugged meaninglessly
and soon found herself
wringing blossoms ruthlessly
and dropping them into the Bay.
(Impatiently, she wondered when he'd have his say)

Suddenly he produced a knife;
she, a giggle.
From a movie, he chose the phrase:
'If I can't have you, no-one will.'
At this she laughed all the harder,
hysterical enough now to laugh at a piece of plain
                                            paper
or the very word 'Don't!'

And then he was upon her
and they were both on the mud
by the Chesapeake.

But he'd flung the knife
and there was no danger in his face —
only fear
and a terrible confusion.

Because he was nineteen,
and male,
and they hadn't seen the same movies.

He helped her up,
she dusted herself off
and they walked stiffly to the road.

No Thanks

I do not thank you
for doing me Good
grandly/loudly/quickly —
and then getting the hell out of the way.
You were already Doing somebody else
while I boiled and shrank your charity
and over-watered your flowering hopes for me.
Funny, but you seemed grateful
I didn't get it right:
you might still be needed.

I do not thank you
for binding my hands
and building a scaffold to my mouth
until all that was as necessary
as the camouflaging dirt on me —
was suborned and sublimated.
I'm left with a horror of smells.

Thank God I'm a disappointment —
no, don't protest:
your praise is galling.
my name in your mouth appals me.
Yes, yes, I know you can't hang around —
what with so much Good to do and all —
and I know that you don't know
of any reason to beg my pardon.
And because you've done me too much damned Good
I'm in danger of begging yours!

You can go — but, hey!
Before you go...
you might at least thank me.

Sündenbock

Squoze together on the front seat, two
Hassidic Jews
shrug wearily.

Displacing the curl of humility
one
adjusts an ear-piece,
cutting out the music
of the pale androgene
in the quilted parka.

The other cringes into
his overcoat,
sniffing obliquely at the dreaming Rasta
across the aisle,
who treads his own Zion,
to judge by his smile.

A man with a water fountain
disguised as a pink pony tail
climbs the stairs
and clinging to the rail,
as the bus jerks,
sprinkles the Jews unknowingly.

I notice they neither look up
or around
and only shyly
wipe away the spray
and this only after
the cord jacket two seats back
has controlled his laughter.

Then, calmly, one de-mists his glasses,
the other re-tunes his hearing aid
as first the androgene
and then the music fade.
Languidly the Rasta rises
still smiling conspiratorially.
In his wake a hissing startles me:
'Schwartze!'

Ashamed. I reach for and close around
the Yiddish for 'scapegoat'.

Plaza On The Park

In the hotel bar
the two to my left are
speaking Dutch
the two to my right
double dutch.
I want to be
somewhere else but
it's 1.30 a.m. —
my train was late.
I missed the complimentary meal.
The common bottle of beer costs £1.50
but the common fly
still stalks the art nouveau
table.

Laugh

I laugh in my sleep
In his, he is pursued.
Waking, I rub his back:
Come morning, he never remembers.

SUA HUAB

Ode To A Bigot (Make Way For Our Liberation)

i
I don't want you to look at me
I'll hide myself away.
I don't want you to harass me
So I'll go my own way.
I promise you I'll be so quiet
And I'll never show
My feelings of anxiety and resentment, no
I'll never bother you
I promise I'll be good
I'll never ever ask of you
More than I should

ii
But why should I behave like this?
Why can't I be free?
This face that I am seeing is different,
But it's me!
Why can't I just have my say,
And tell you how I pain?
Why can't I shout out aloud
And tell you all again?
I won't be silenced anymore —
My patience has run out!
You make me feel so sick inside
Because you never doubt
Your absolute authority

iii
(and now this starts to show)
Your views are going to ruin you,
But with them I will grow.
The only consolation of the way
You feel for me,
Is the fact that I have freedom
and free you'll never be.
Your bigotry is your lifeline,
Prejudice is your source,
Such blindness is so trying
and leaves no time for remorse.
I'll even offer pity
Because you feel this way
But make way for my liberation
In this state I won't stay.
Make way for our liberation,
We'll free you if we may.

Next Please

Who are you?
My name is...
Where are you from?
I come from...
Where have you been?
Well I ...
What do you do?
I am...
(We don't really care,) but;
Just write your name
On the dotted line.
We'll put you on file with
The rest of our numbers.
What do you want here?
I want, well...
I just want.

You

You live
In a white-walled city
And have
White-washed opinions
And feel nothing.

You have
Clear cut conceptions
Of the situation
And you feel nothing.

You use
Diseased definition
To describe discrimination
You feel nothing.

You guide
Glib generalisations
Towards painful operations
And feel nothing.

But

You live
In a white-walled city
So have white-washed opinions
We know
Your misguided conceptions
Lead to misinterpretations
And diseased definition
Aids disaster.

Although you feel
Nothing
We feel
Despite your indifference

We feel
We feel
We feel.

LORNA EUPHEMIA GRIFFITHS

Give and Take

We let them into our lands
and were stolen.
They let us into their lands
to give them what they needed.
They returned to our lands and swapped
their poor mimicry for our genuinity.
They returned to their lands
and imposed sick immigration laws.
But we demanded attention
and they welcomed our attention
to learn and re-teach us
telling us that hating them for their perverted
existence of exploitation
was racist.
And we took it and surfaced and
let them into our hearts
still serving them
And they still take us.
But we don't exist
with and for them
Fuck the shared communication
of give and take.

JOLINA BLACK

I'm Not Sure

I'm not sure where we went wrong
Or why our love just grew apart
And the way he treated me it's as if he hadn't
a heart.
I'm not sure why his soft touch of tenderness
turned to grips of stone
or why, many many nights he went out and left
me all alone.
Whenever he wanted money he'd call me his true
love and honey bunch
But if I had no money, honey was watered down
to bitch and a heavy punch.
I'm not sure why he turned on me, it could've
been drugs, maybe drinks, but it's not a proper
excuse to treat someone without any respect.
He tried to make me a nervous wreck.
So when he went out of that door
I'm not sure why I didn't feel sore
But I'm damn sure I don't want him back
anymore.

Ebony Baby Girl

It was half past one
When my pain began.
I could hardly stand up.
and I couldn't sit down.
The way I was walking, I felt like a clown.
I looked at Den, he was ever so calm,
he thought it was just another false alarm.
Then I bawled,
Well he never heard me bawl like that
before.
Next thing I knew he ran out of the door.
I'm sure his feet didn't touch the floor.
I rided the pain until the ambulance
came.
We finally reached the hospital
and they rushed me inside.
The nurses laid me on a bed and opened my
legs up wide.
I shouted, 'please give me something, the
pain's getting worse'.
Den looked at me and said, 'I thought
you wanted natural birth'.
Well I could have cursed,
but instead I shouted 'nurse!'
She said she couldn't give me anything
'because the baby's head is coming at last,
and if I wanted I could have gas'.
Well I breathed in that gas, until I was high.
And all I could hear was a frail little cry.
My body was shaking, my head in a whirl.
By the time I came round
Lying between my breasts was a beautiful
ebony baby girl.

GEORGINA A. BLAKE

Identity Parade

'This is not me' I wanted to say
Though I know him exceptionally well
Sure enough he has my looks
And he walks as I in trips and starts
But he has been known to kiss and tell
Which is something I would never do.

There is only one of me
There has to be — for my mother
always said
She has to be right
She always wins
'Listen — this is not me'
I wanted to shout.

I'm a good worker and straight home
to the wife
I'm not the one to lurk in doorways
Or hide behind trees and wait for the
Unsuspecting as they travel alone at night.

I'm happy, well adjusted
And I had a good childhood
Never deprived of books and the best toys.
I ate chewing gum in class once
But that's all — 'I'm me — not him'
I wanted to scream — at this my
impossible dream.

He was always the one — him
Masquerading as I — summoned
When trouble arrived like an unwanted guest.
'It has to be him — it is not me'
I wanted to say — but I did not
As they singled me out of the
identity parade, clicked the
handcuffs shut and took me away

Yellow...

The coward
Ran away and hid in the long grass
While her friends did the fighting
For the things she believed in

When the fracas was over
She found she had grown
Fat on her fear
She could no longer stand
Or support her bloated
Custardy body;
So she sat down again
And began to write diets
Of bravery and fine speeches
These would make her thin
And accepted; all would forget
Her yellow malaise

Meanwhile her friends had
gone searching — they wanted
to tell her their war had been won.

When
She was discovered
Her grassy home
Had been burned away by the light
Of the sun
It had turned to hay
And she had become fodder
For those who thrive on protecting the weak.

Coffee Morning at Your House

And I might just call and say hello
if the sun comes out and we're
blessed with warmth
For half a day or more
For my heart will be light
And troubles seem slight
So I might just call and say hello.

Look for me then
Wait for me then
Have the kettle to the boil
And we'll make some tea
And talk of the past
As we eat the cakes that I'll bring.

Forget the mess the others have made
All in good time — let's make time
Among the washing and pans
For I shall be gone in an hour or so
If I should call and say hello
And I just might.

Before all this
Do you remember
How we roomed together long ago?
Have we changed the world?
Have we had the time?
We did before all this.

Then came marriage and children first
And the ship it sank
Before we were saved
Caught up in the waves of life.

But we've this time to spend
So we do sometimes
Share reminiscences at a coffee morning
at your house.

Driftwood

I	II	III
Love	She	She
like	wished	wished
driftwood	to	to
washed	be	become
up	taken	part
on	and	of
the	made	a
beach	into	mantlepiece
waited	a	or
for	sculpture	a
someone	that	rosebowl
to	many	she
find	would	wished
her	admire	to
		be
		adorned

Entertain Me With Love Stories

Cries of my brother
Shatter the air
And the stillness and blue
Of the summer's destroyed
By the tears and despair
But the pain is not mine
So I'll keep my ear to the ground
And I'll turn a blind eye
For I've burdens enough in my life
No-one else wants to share.

So why should I have
Any regard for their weeping?
Why should I be moved by emotion
When I see the dead and the dying
In the townships
On dusty roads
In broken corrugated iron shacks?

It's immoral to have them strewn
Across my TV screen
Entice me with tempting products to buy
Entertain me with love stories and comedy even
But don't make my heart
Scream in silence
At my shame for living a fortunate life
Away from apartheid.

If the truth must be told
I'm embarrassed by my
Black curly hair
And my skin which is the same
As those unpaid stars of the
Nine O'clock news.

How little I suffer
Yet I must sit and watch
The distress and frustration
In the faces of those I will never meet
Or else ignore them.

Is it any wonder
I bury my head in the sand?

How can I stop the relentless
Injustice ?

By observing a people degraded?

No —
My awareness alters nothing.

Apartheid lives — just as
God saves his believers?

Crossing Bridges

naked
without
purpose
this
poem
has
no
form
idea or meaning

yet it lives

like
crossing
bridges
leads
us
to
our
destiny

NAYABA AGHEDO

Invasion

For ten thousand years
We survived
We built our cities
We built our pride
And then you came
Like a thief in the night
And stole all you could
That was ours by right
You came with your guns
                        your bible
                            your beads

You raped our lands
And neglected our needs

In 400 years
You tried to destroy our race
You made poverty and famine commonplace

White rule we remember
Dead slaves, they still cry
Our blood still builds your banks
And our babies, they still die

But listen now fat Whiteman
Wipe the blood from your eyes
AFRIKA is angry
And now she will arise

Your victims want their revenge
It's long overdue
And nothing will stop them
Until they're paid in full, by YOU

Bad Hair

Bad hair
If it ain't slick and oily
It's bad hair
If it's not called Gerry or Hollywood,
Supercurl or Wurly-Wurl
It's bad hair
If ain't relaxed to your knees
Or don't take off in a breeze
Hell then child, it's bad hair

Don't want no 'Tough' head in my family albums
No microphone head blocking out my face at a
blues
No!
I want flowing, glowing,
                    shining, winding,
                         long,
Fried hair!

Then one day, I woke up, lifted my head
And my hair stayed on the pillow!
With one inch left,
Why girl! I had to love my natural, bouncy,
Beautiful African remainder.
I plaited, it grew
I cornrowed, so long
I braided, Hmm! what a picture Cleopatra!

Now, I ain't no wet-head
No chemical smash hit
I don't walk around with no fire hazard on my
                                        head
I'm just natural, proud
And glad.

Fool's Gold

He sports gold on his hands
Hmmm, diamonds on his fingers
Yeah, he sure does look like Marvin
Boy, he's a deadringer!

Sweet talk, love, sex and lust
Girl, he promised you
Politics should be his game
Pulls off one damn coup

Transfixed by his deep brown eyes
Shining bright and bad
The danger, thrills
They promised you
Almost drove you mad

Well
Child
Are you sorry now
Left with babe and all
Mama said 'Watch out for men'
But you were bound to fall

Mesmerised by his FLASH
Gold
    Car
       Coooool flat
Riches you gave
Worth much more
You can't have your love back

I'm not here to judge you
You say you know your mind
Don't look for wealth
That is false
Check out his bottom line.

Bloodties

My Son
My Brother
My Father

Why in images of war
Do I see your face

Why on foreign battlefields
Do I recognise your body

Why are you there
Why are you fighting
For a people who
                    in peacetime anyway
Don't even acknowledge
Your right to
              Eat their grain
                    To walk their roads
                          Or man the system

Back home
Veiled black mother
Mourns your loss

But I
A sister — but unknown to you
Have no time for grief

Just anger
That they sent you
Anger
That you went

In the heat of Korea
You didn't feel
My cool hand
Holding you back

In 'Nam
Didn't you hear me calling 'No'...?

Now in South Africa
It is I
Still holding
Still calling
Who stands over
Your body
And washes it
With bitter tears

ANNETTE REIS

Child In Me

I remember a summer day
and heat haze that lay still above the ground.
Muffled laughter and tar that bubbled between
                                    cobble stones.
Jock, the mongrel, his hair stiff grey-white. I smell
                                    him warm and doggy,
I feel the lick of his tongue on my skin.
I see me.
I run down the thin-carpeted hallway of my
                                    grandmother's house.
My sandals are white with crepe soles thick and
                                    creamy, stitched to
softest leather, their buckles glinting up at me.
I remember summer — 1949
I am three years old.

The Dream

Dark crowds below a window.
Some kind of riot.
My son.
He climbs over the theatre audience
But the seats are made of crumbling fungi
They break at each stride.
I protect him;
I build a set with black sugar paper.
I use optical illusion to create atmosphere.
I show it to my daughter,
She says
'The world is so constructed that the 'Penny
                              Thoory' never fails -
everything that is borrowed must therefore be
                                        repaid.'
My friend.
I say a last goodbye and wake
To unshed tears

SALLY NEASER

The Illegitimate Child

I am the one you left behind.
I am the one you spurned.
When you walked away from me
You never knew the tables would turn.

I thought I was the one to blame
For you leaving me.
I did not see as a child nor understand
Why you didn't want me.

You were never there when I needed love.
You were never there when mum needed support.
You weren't there to share my achievements
When I won a trophy for school sport.

You say you were too young for a child.
Be honest, you just didn't care.
If you were too young to be a father
You shouldn't have put me there.

You were old enough to sleep with my mother.
You were old enough to prove you were a man.
Now you're the one not being loved.
Catch me, if you can.

Now your hair is grey and thinning.
Your eyesight is fading too.
I am the one you want now.
I am the one who doesn't want you.

Would He?

I would love a man to carry a child
And feel its movements as I do.
Would he want to extinguish the life
The way he expects me to?

Being A Woman

I was clothed in fine frilly dresses
With ribbons and bows in my hair,
Looking a bit like an Easter Bunny.
I was young and didn't care.

At five I wouldn't wear them.
T-shirts and jeans were my attire then.
My mother said 'You're too big for a vest,'
and bought me a bra when I was ten.

The freedom of my vest I longed
For I and bras just don't agree.
The hooks and straps irritated my skin.
I felt trapped and wanted to be free.

My pains started when I was about thirteen.
'You're a woman. Ah. That's sweet.'
'Yes mum. Wonderful isn't it?'
Holding my stomach with blood on my sheet.

'Now at last you're a woman
You must cook, clean and do it well.'
'Yes mum,' I said with the beam in my eye.
Now is the time to rebel.

'It wasn't just me,' I said to her,
'Why make all this fuss?
The way you go on you'd think I'd robbed a bank
I've only hijacked a school bus.'

I was frightened to tell her at first
— You know, what I just did.
'Why can't you tell me you're pregnant like all the
                                other girls?'
And she wasn't too pleased when I did.

Childbirth is a wonderful thing,
A teacher to me once said.
I remember thinking that as I laid there
With the ankles at the back of my head.

You will suffer bearing children.
God, you certainly wasn't wrong.
It only takes ten minutes on the telly
I didn't realise it would have been that long.

When I took my son home and looked in the mirror
I could've broken down and cried.
Stretch marks bright red look at me.
I felt ugly and wanted to die.

I'm not having any more children.
I'll go with the dog to the vet.
It's a curse being a woman,
I've got the menopause to look forward to yet.

LORRAINE GRIFFITHS

Home Truths

I offered

the grey woman my seat

Cos

her wrinkles had already learned

to

grow

tired

With silver spools riveted to her head

by a scarf that had swathed

too many washing lines

Flowers bleached

by the drudge of time

She looked

at

me

Mouth taut as a queue in a storm

She didn't whisper

Thank you.

and spray sunshine through plastic teeth

Cos

The son of her son

had

   popped

        dog

          shit

Through a 'paki's' letterbox

the day before

GLORIA KNOWLES

Past and Present

I do remember you mother,
Light in my soul guiding me through.
Darkness took hold when your limbs were cold;
Dead and soon to be buried you filled your coffin.

Smiles were once upon that face.
I left you contented with nothing else to unfold.
All that was left in your mind was to bury the pain,
Even if that meant closing off the future as well.

Never distant from my thoughts;
My mind I have given to you to live on in.
Things are said to me, so a character like you I
                                        will to be.
Strong, motherly, wise and honest; I cannot
                        summon a performance.

I am what I am, not a patch on you.
I could not have bared or borne what you did.
Solemnly in depression I crave for your presence,
Eager to recapture the happy times we had.

Release

Release, please release, release this rummaging
infestation in my head.
Prize open the scar glowing from under Black
plaited hair, synthetic of course.
Look into the centre, the mind, my core.
Poetry, business, child, fiancé, money, friends
and work all intermingled.
Where does one end and another begin? I cannot
answer.
Trying to do one's best, but at that dreaded time of
the month being rational does not come into play.
So one glass of wine to get tipsy and another to
get giddy drowns out all my brain to leave a zombie
to giggle, laugh and fall back into a moment's sleep.
Aha no more pain, until tomorrow when life begins
again.

Today I Laughed

I actually laughed today.
At work; I actually laughed.

Days gone by stress, tension and
Old age pains would hit me.
Me?

At twenty six, no twenty five,
Silly how my memory fails me,
I had my first sauna.

Does working with old people
Slow your mind down, or would it
Be more slow if I didn't work?

Come off it, I'm young and, and,
And, and, and — getting older.

Oh I'd nearly forgotten I laughed
At work today, and I feel great.

I feel great, I feel great
— I feel great?

PAULINE OMOBOYE

Look At Me

Look at me —
Go on look at me
I dare you to look at me, what can you see?
A woman who's lost her virginity?
Someone footloose, fancy and free?
Well —
Look at me
I'm asking you nicely
Just analyse my structure and poise
I'm not just a Black woman who's hurting
Or shouting creating a noise
I-am-woman.
And I'm aching all over
'From the outside right through to my bones
I'm crying
I'm shaking
I'm angry
I'm emotionally torn deep inside
No longer can I hide my feelings
And think only of my pride

Look at me.
I dare you to look straight into my eyes
There's no suprise
No hatred
No shame

Just pity, pity
Pity for those who remain ignorant purely by choice
Whom because they're happy and secure they ask
for no more
I do —
I'm asking you.
Keep up the good fight
Help us all to unite
Keep up the struggle for emancipation so all
women can be free

I'm *liberated*
And it's clear to see
Because I am me.

Go on look at me.

Innocent Victim

The disfigured body of a sister was found
She was brutally battered and tossed to the ground
she was left to die...
no-one heard her cries...
and somewhere sits an animal
who calls himself a *man*
cunning in his disappearance
blood-stained hands
I just can't understand

It's almost unbelievable although it's clear to see
something drastic needs to happen in this society

Once again an innocent woman
was the victim of a murderer
someone...
somewhere...
someone must have heard her
her sisters sit and quiver
for this killer we must deliver
he's degrading
we must erase him
from our society

All the conferences and meetings
have still not found this criminal
people *move to action*
to allow justice her will
find the killer...
find the killer...
let us walk with our heads high
not sit waiting for another one of our sisters to die

We're too lenient to these maniacs
we need justice for these thugs

we're not playthings, we are *women*
not just here to be raped or mugged
Just because we feel like dancing
and we go out all alone
It doesn't mean we're looking for a man to take us
home
It doesn't mean we're crazy
and it sure don't mean we're mad
we are women...and we're human
not just here for men to have.

Find the killer

Black and Beautiful

Mummy can you tell me something true?
Is there something special about me and you?
Are we like Martians who come from space?
Why do people stare at me in disgrace?

My hair is combed,
My clothes are smart,
My teeth are sparkling white,
My shoes they shine,
The school bag's mine,
My trousers not too tight.

Mummy can you tell me something, can I ask you true?
Is there something special about me and you?

Son, listen carefully you're perfect and you're
bright
The only thing that you don't have is the colour
skin that's white
That's why they think you're different
The facts are clear and true
Being Black is beautiful
Like perfect little you.

KANTA WALKER

Black Sister

Black sister
I haven't seen for a full year
Rushes up to me
Like a long lost friend
Gives me a firm hug
And a peck on the cheek.
(Very English —
Not much of the East in such gestures!)

I return her affection
Guilt ridden, ashamed
Why didn't I give her the greetings first?
She must think of me
Horribly cold!

I offer her some tea
With three spoons of sugar
To compensate...

'Life is hard', she starts
'Under this racist regime.
Thatcherite bastards want us out, out.
See what is happening to Viraj Mendis!
Yes, they want us out!'
With vehemence she pronounces.

'Come to our March the 8th Meeting.
At this crucial time in our history
We need solidarity.'

Then she pushes a piece of crumpled paper
Under my nose —
'These are the sisters I have invited
To organise the day.
I know some of them are headstrong,
Quick to challenge and fight among themselves.
Some of them are competitive and
Wish to be the Nouveau leaders.
But it is only for a day.
We should give them more rope.
We old ones can afford to
It is only for a day.
Come lend me your support for solidarity
For Black sisters
It is only for a day!'

'I would, I would try,
I would come, of course,
Of course, it is only for a day',
I limply say.

She pecks my cheek again, hugs perfunctorily
and departs looking for another sister
Who regards
Love and solidarity among Black sisters
Another game to be played
In front of well meaning, white audiences!

Anger

Anger lingers
Keeps me awake
In the fullness
Of a stillmoon night.

Anger gnaws pitilessly
At the pit of my stomach
Acid rises and burns holes
In forgiveness.

Anger billows and blasts
Gathers momentum
And volume
It grows as it feeds
On my unspent rage.

Anger wants an eruption
Enough to shake
Many ships
And drown —

Injustices, cruelties,
Inequalities
Which jolt my memory daily
And remind me
Of the universal hurt
Humiliation, pain.

When Did You Cry Last?

When did you cry last? — he asked me,
Gentle, kind man with golden hair
And cornflower blue eyes uplifted waits
For the answer to merge his pain with mine!

'I don't know...I never cry — not much!'

Should I have told him that I dare not cry
For my cries will, if unleashed
Render oceans apart, become hurricanes,
Seething earthquakes, violent volcanoes,
And turn this world upside down in utter agony!

What should I cry for?
Should I cry for Palestine, Lebanon, Eritrea,
Nicaragua, South Africa, Ethiopia, Ireland,
Chile, El Salvador, Iraq, Iran or my own land?

Should I cry for autocrats, bureaucrats, plutocrats,
Aristocrats, Socialists, Communists,
Anarchists, Thatcherite Capitalists,
Or for Barbarians, Military Dictators or
For the oppressive nature of greed, power and
domination?

Should I cry for my rape? — rape within marriage
Rape without marriage? Rape of my country?
By the British, by Americans, by others
Who rule by the bomb and the gun,
Who violate my brothers and my sisters?

Should I weep for the lack of love in my life?
Should I weep for centuries of subjugation?
For slavery, exploitation and the pain
Of hunger, starvation and humiliation?

Should I weep for my Love who abandoned me?
And is now in chains in his land — my

                                        homeland?
Don't ask me when I cried last — Brother!
My tears will be a fearful sight to see
They may tear you apart and smash your sensitive
Heart to SMITHEREENS.

Upon Nature Of Man

On a hot August night
When the house is empty and hollow
It beats like a drum and reverberates
With the monotonous roar of
Passing automobile engines,
It hums like a beehive.

I lie still and think
About the nature of husbands!
How, fitful his temperament!
His passions are so much attuned
To the automobile engines —
It roars away when filled with gasoline,
Takes wing and only
The dull roar is left behind!

So men take off from women
When the novelty of sex is satiated.
And women like so many sad Eves
Nurse in privacy their broken hearts,
Still trying harder to remember
Their youth of yesterday
And seek comfort in 'motherhood.'
While men roar, and race
Like so many automobiles
From petrol pump to petrol pump
Till metal fatigue sets in
And their bodies are the property of the scrapyard
Their beloved homes!

They seek refuge and comfort in mowing lawns
And tidying up garden sheds.
Their wives now mellowed by old age and
                                        patience,

Ever forgiving, and forgetting
Never, ever remembering the dreams
And ideals they once had
Of eternal love and faithfulness.
They forgive and forget and toast their trespasses
With endless cups of sugared tea and biscuits,
And talk about their grandchildren!

The Right Mix

We must have the mix right, she said
With a twinkle in her eye.
3 Whites, 1.5 West Indians and 1.4 Asians
That's what our requirements are
To make our Project viable
And to give it credibility.

Furthermore, we must promote the cause
The ethnic minorities — I mean the Blacks.
That's why we must have 1.5 West Indians,
1.4 Asians to 3 White workers —
To get the mix right,
And fight for the Cause!
After all Britain is a multi-racial society
And we are here to see justice done!

That's why I am prepared to work for no wages
Because I believe in the CAUSE.
My expenses do help me to run the car
And pay for my telephone
But compared to what others get
They are peanuts!

Do come and work for us, Sister
For you will help us greatly
And get our ratio right.

After she had left
I reflected — I recognise
The face of the New Ruling Class
The one that wants the mix right
For a multi-racial Britain —
Is prepared to make sacrifices
To work only for expenses
For *a Good Cause.*

Trunk Call

Remote — Distant
Stuttered, staggered
With time lapse
Of the continents to connect —
For the sound that travels so fast.
I cling on desperately
To catch ping-pong, jumpy
Disjointed words
Of the trunk call —
Spanning the Indian Ocean
Through Bahrain Straits
The Gulf — I can see strings of words
Travelling through air and then hitting
My lap on a Friday afternoon —
Language of reassurance —
Of remoteness — of distance —
I clutch at it
For comfort.
Imbibing meaning
And profundity to
The everyday — ordinary
And banal —
Of a Friday afternoon
Trunk Call.

Raising Of Lazarus

Since I had my consciousness raised
I have come to think differently
About myself.

You will have to be patient
He said.
Then I can tell you what it was
All about!

There were eight of us in all
For a whole weekend
And we learnt about ourselves
How not to think
In stereotyped sex roles
As men.
But be people first.

Parts of this introspection
Have been painful but
It has done me good.

You will have to be patient
And wait, and I would
Tell you all about it!

Women have to be patient
And wait, when men have
Their consciousness raised.
Patience is not a virtue,
Death comes to the patient.

STORIES

CARLENE MONTOUTE

Simmy

Every hour on the hour, a ferry boat leaves the pierhead and takes its passengers to neighbouring destinations across the River Mersey. For the children, going 'over the water' is a big adventure. In New Brighton there is a funfair to explore with candy-striped rock to buy, enough to guarantee an aching stomach. Nearby, In Meols, when the tide goes out, children and adults scramble across the rocks and fill their buckets with cueins. These are taken home, boiled in salt water and eaten. The proper name for this shellfish is Whelk but nobody here ever calls it that. On Harrison Drive beach sandcastles are built and photographs taken before the contents of the picnic basket is devoured. The journey home finds most children subdued, as they rest their weary bodies onto the even wearier bodies of their parents. They stare in a daze as the boat approaches the pierhead. They can see the familiar clock-faced building where two eighteen feet metal birds sit and watch. This, the Liver Building, is the symbolic trademark which welcomes the travellers back to their home — the City of Liverpool.

At the pierhead, the docks divide the city into north and south. There is a street which runs between Brunswick and Toxteth Docks. This takes you through to the Southend, first to the area of Dingle, then into Toxteth. But nobody here ever calls it that. It is simply known as Liverpool 8 — a great big melting pot of faces, shapes, colours, sizes and races. Simone had spent all of her life here. This eight year old child could not imagine living anywhere else.

It was an early Sunday evening when the last ferry boat returned from its journey. The de Jonge family gathered their belongings and quickly made their way home. On arrival, Simone and her sister were put into the bath where they were washed from top to toe. Simone was always amazed at the amount of sand which found its way to the bottom of the bath. She touched her hair and smiled. This time she was careful not to get any sand in it which meant that it didn't need to be washed again. Simone didn't like to have her hair washed at all but if there was one thing she disliked even more, it was having her hair brushed. She would cry out in pain as it tried to disentangle the confused mass, which couldn't take a comb. It was a daily ordeal which Simone hated. Her mother would take a handful of grease which was vigorously rubbed into the hair and scalp. Simone was told that this would make the brushing process easier. Easier for whom she wondered. She still felt the pain, and her mother still cursed and had beads of sweat on her face.

Then, a hot comb was used, to make her hair more 'manageable'. Still a daily ordeal for mother and child. The heavy metal comb would be put onto the stove where it would glow red with the heat. When it was removed it was gently swept through the hair making it temporarily straight. The hair would then be plaited. Sometimes Simone would fidget, as if she had an itch which couldn't be soothed by scratching. This usually resulted in a burn to the neck or ear and a sharp telling off from her mother for not keeping still.

One day at school she was asked by her teacher about the mark on her neck.

'My mum burnt me Miss.' It was said in a manner that was very matter of fact. Simone couldn't understand her mother's anger when the teacher requested to see her.

On the way home her mother held her hand so tight, Simone thought that she was going to faint.

'Why didn't you tell your teacher I was hot combing your hair? You've caused me more than enough trouble girl. I do my best and look what happens. The cheek of the woman, thinking I could abuse my own child. If you'd have kept your head still in the first place you wouldn't have got burnt. Why wasn't you born with decent hair like your sister?' Simone knew that this wasn't a question to be answered. And if there was an answer, she didn't know it. Her eyes filled with tears. She hadn't realised that her mother would get into trouble. She wanted to ask what the word abuse meant — but her mother's anger kept her silent. Eyes stinging, she fought hard not to cry. Her hand hurt, so did her heart. She hated her hair. It caused so much trouble.

One day Simone arrived home from school to be told that after the weekend, her hair would never be hot combed again. She was to have it 'processed'. Her mother's voice was filled with excitement as she explained about the new straightening technique.

'It's from the United States of America. Mind you, they know what they're doing over there. They know how to deal with our type of hair, especially difficult hair like yours Simmy. Once it's processed, it doesn't need to be done again for three or four months.'

As she lay in bed, Simone tried to imagine what she would look like with processed hair. It wasn't easy.

On Sunday morning Simone was up early. Washed, dressed and fed, she and her sister sat on the step of the front door, eagerly awaiting the arrival of her saviour.

Mid-morning he arrived with a smile and a large cardboard box. He presented the girls with a shiny half crown coin each. They glanced at their mother, who nodded that it was fine to accept the money. As the sisters chattered about the various sweets they would buy, the man addressed their mother.

'Eva, you're lookin' fine girl.'
She gave a little laugh and showed him into the living room, where her husband was. Simone decided that she liked the man. Not because he had given them money, and not because he was going to process her hair. She liked his smile. Her mother told her that his name was Cye.

'He's your father's countryman. He's just opened his own hairdressing salon. Simmy, your hair's going to look so good. Just imagine; no more hot combing; no more sweating.'

At quarter to eleven, the operation began. Simone's hair was washed with a sweet smelling shampoo which reminded her of the caramel pudding her mother sometimes made on Sundays. She hoped that her mother made the pudding today.

Cye chatted to her father about 'back home'. Simone often wondered why she, her mother and sister had been born in this cold, wet country. She remembered the day she'd been watching the television, patiently waiting for the news broadcast to end. The newscaster began to talk about 'coloured' people then a picture of an airport appeared on the screen. He mentioned a word which Simone hadn't heard before and which she couldn't pronounce properly. She asked her mother what it meant. Her mother explained that 'indigenous' meant 'belonging naturally'.

'The way we do Simmy, because we're British born black people.'

The shampoo bottle went back into the cardboard box, and out came a pair of yellow rubber gloves and a tub of cream. Her sister, who was perched on the edge of her chair, watched the procedure in earnest. Simone craned her neck for a better examination of the tub.

She thought that it looked like the Brylcreem which was displayed in the chemist shop window.

Gloves on, Cye scooped out a handful of the cream. Her mother gave a reassuring smile as she said. 'Simmy, that's the cream that'll make your hair nice and straight. Keep very still now.'

Simone nodded and closed her eyes as the dollop of cream came crashing down onto her head. It was cold, and it smelt awful, just like the cream her Aunt Marjie used to remove the hair from her legs. Cye applied more cream and rubbed it into the hair and scalp, until Simone's head was completely covered. Her sister giggled, then quickly put her hand to her mouth as she received a serious look from her mother. Simone felt her scalp tingle. Seconds later, there was an incredible burning sensation, as if her head were on fire. She began to cry. Her mother tried to comfort her.

'Simmy, the cream needs to be left on for half an hour. Isn't it worth a little bit of pain for beautiful hair?'

Simone nodded miserably. Her mother dabbed at her eyes with a handkerchief. The photograph album was produced to try and take Simone's mind off the pain. She usually loved to look at the album, as her mother always had a story to tell about each photograph. This time, not even the album could help Simone to forget about the burning on her scalp.

After what seemed an eternity, the cream was washed from Simone's hair. Tears welled up again. She had never felt such relief.

Another bottle was taken from the box and the contents squeezed onto Simone's head. It smelt of coconut. This, she was told, would help to soothe her scalp. The hair was towel dried gently. Cye gave a laugh of self admiration as he combed the hair with such ease.

'Yes man. It's taken good.'

Simone put her hands to her head. The sores on her scalp paled into insignificance as she fingered the hair. It felt as thin and straight as the bristles on the pastry brush her mother used when baking. She looked at her mother who smiled. Her sister stared in amazement, then asked if she could touch it. Her father glanced up from his newspaper and gave a nod of approval. And Cye. Well, he grinned like a cat that had got the cream. The suspense was too much for Simone. She jumped up from her chair and ran into the lobby. At last she would see for herself. She stood, eyes closed, in front of the mirror. On the count of ten, she opened them and gasped in disbelief. She had a headful of hair that was so straight it looked like strands of black cotton.

'Well Simmy?' Her mother stood in the doorway.

Simone smiled as she thought about the various ways she could have her new hair. A pony tail; maybe bunches — or simply hanging loose.

Simone's heart felt good.

Her hair problems were finally over...

But this little girl didn't realise, that her hair problems had only just begun.

LORNA EUPHEMIA GRIFFITHS

Irretrievable Breakdown

The cold sheets, cruel and uninviting, rubbed icily against my curled bare legs. I tried to pull my night-shirt down, stretching it until I heard the seams creak. I tried to turn over, trying not to venture an inch outside the warm patch directly beneath me, which the pressure of my curled body had created. The wind hissed outside the window, the leaves and branches snapping in song. I tucked the duvet even further under my chin.

I had left the landing light on because I was afraid of the dark. I had been afraid of the dark for as long as I could remember. Yes, I could remember the constant nightly nightmares as a child. I would lay there forcing my heavy eyelids to stay open, not daring to fall asleep, to offer myself mercilessly to the crabby clutches of the large monstrous figures... I shivered. The distorted shadow of the chair over in the corner with clothes thrust lazily upon it eerily resembled one of those friends of the night right now, and I blinked trying to focus my eyes on the red light filtering through the narrow space at the top of the bedroom door.

Devon loved the dark, he seemed to always come alive at night time. He'd spend all day in a mindless stupor slumped in front of the television and as soon as night came he was quick witted and lively and charming. I can remember the day I met him, well actually it was night. I was having a well earned night out and as I danced freely, swinging and swaying back and forth, glass perched unsteadily in my raised hand, a tall dark frame passed closely in front of me and the inevitable happened. Brandy and Babycham peppered his smart grey suit.

'Sorry!' I spluttered.

'It's alright,' he smiled, revealing a perfect set of even white teeth. He had big brown eyes and long curly eyelashes — a bit baby cute I thought but nonetheless very attractive. Later on he had asked me to dance and as I danced — not too close, but close enough to make contact — I noticed that he was the owner of a strong looking pair of very broad shoulders! As we swayed rhythmically to the soulful tunes of Ken Boothe, the smoke in the atmosphere pricked my eyes and I found myself trying to shield them by way of burying my head into his damp shirted chest. I had since been coolly unavailable for successive dates and then I hadn't heard from him for months. I was afraid that I had unintentionally frightened him off and so when I bumped into him in a busy food store, despite the fact that I hadn't done my hair or got my face on, I invited him over for dinner.

I shivered and tugged again at the duvet as the wind howled, losing to the sudden competitive screech of the local owl. The leaves replied with a wicked rustling crescendo whilst the heavy branches continued to swish and sway. The luminous numbers of the digital clock on the crowded bedside table reminded me that I had been lying in bed for almost an hour and still sleep eluded me. I leaned across and put the radio on in order to rid the night of its silence.

Devon liked to listen to the radio in bed. At first I didn't mind it, and sometimes quite enjoyed the extra company, but as time went on I hated the voices and the music and the jingles and the intrusion. I had longed for the warmth and quietness of Devon's undivided attention. He had been so loving, so spoiling yet the years had changed him. It had started on that day. The day he had been forced to join the ranks of the forgotten millions. At first it was like a holiday. The long days and nights together were welcomed as we clambered out of bed in the late afternoon after feasting on love and laughter for breakfast and dinner, but the excitement had waned and the novelty became a mechanical routine. Soon the laughter stopped and we'd get up as soon as it was light. The repeated refusals of each job application sabotaged Devon's energy and sense of humour. I increasingly became irritated by his very presence day after day and the bickering set in.

'Why can't you put things away when you've finished with them?' I'd start.

'If it bothers you that much put them away yourself,' he'd answer.

I noticed how he slurped his tea and ate noisily; he'd leave the wet towel hanging over the side of the bath; I'd cringe at the way he always left the empty cup at the side of the chair where he was sitting; at night when he undressed he'd roll his socks into a ball and toss them onto the chair; I hated him for becoming listless and square eyed.

The warm caresses became cool and the laughter mere smiles. He accused me of not understanding, after all he had worked solidly as an engineer for the past eight years. He had come to take for granted the security and the lifestyle that a good job with good wages had brought him. But that comfort seemed so distant now. He took solace in the television by day and when we were alone at night he would try to hide his thoughts by falsely occupying himself with the radio. We became as distant as the good times, but I loved him. I loved to look at him. We would be in the middle of an argument and all of a sudden I'd see his large soft eyes and full lips and prickly square jaw, the tall broad frame so inviting, and in an instant we had made up and resolved our differences. Why couldn't I have seen then what the future held for us?

As the aimless days sucked away at his self esteem he had somehow blamed me. He was forced to rely on me and he hated it. He resented my work, he resented his position of inferiority, he resented the role reversal. And so he tried to punish me. My work was ridiculed and scorned. My person was mocked and belittled, I hurt deeply with the constant verbal insults. I put up with the abuse because I sympathised. It wasn't his fault that he found himself in that unfortunate position, he did try desperately to get out of it. I promised myself that if things worked out I'd do my best to make up for the torment that he had suffered. He had succeeded in making me feel guilty. The rain tapped lightly against the protesting window pane. I turned on my side towards the radio. The warmth beneath the duvet had slowly enveloped my body. I uncurled my legs and stretched my pointed toes to the end of the bed. I turned the volume a shade higher and realised that it was a weak attempt at trying to ignore what was eating my mind.

The red light was no longer a narrow beam above the door as it opened wearily.

'Can't sleep mummy, radio loud.' Marlo rubbed his eyes. Sweet, beautiful little Marlo.

'Oh come here darling. I'm sorry darling. Come, come and keep mummy warm.' Marlo scrambled onto the bed, I pulled back the duvet and helped him under. We hugged, and rubbed, and patted and kissed. I turned the volume down.

'Come on sugar, let's go to sleep'.

Marlo wrapped his soft little limbs fiercely around me, his arm tightly across my neck, the other flung loosely on the empty pillow beside me.

'Bye!' he smiled and closed his eyes.

'Goodnight,' I whispered.

I lay there letting my mind drift back. Devon had got a job and things had been good between us. We crammed ourselves full with sandwiches of love and good living, and then Marlo came. I wanted to believe that things had returned to the way they were in the beginning but I knew in my heart of hearts that the damage had already been done. Devon changed to working the night shift because he earned more money and he felt that it was his way of contributing to the upbringing of his child. He became more and more secretive and selfish — we didn't share our thoughts and things like we used to. It was as though he wanted to hold onto his things for himself, he felt threatened if he felt I knew too much about him. And so we loved each other distantly. When Marlo was happily tottering on his own I went out to work as a journalist for a local newspaper. We needed the money and I needed the space. I had lost myself so easily amongst the endless piles of disposable nappies — replacing my yearning for independence with the yearning for motherhood. I felt I had lost control of my life, I resented being forced into a limited role, and found it more important now to hold onto myself. I was relieved to return to work and equally excited to rush home in the evening to meet that smiling dependant little face.

Devon and I were too tired for each other. Our laughter was sparse. At the weekends we over indulged our son and would fall exhaustedly into bed at night time. Devon still loved the weekend rave-ups and usually went out alone. The weekdays, we passed each other like two ships in the night, the empty feelings of guilt and blame splintering our private times together.

Marlo kicked me sharply in the ribs. I gently moved

him over to the other side of the bed. The red light shone freely in through the open door onto his face. He looked very much like his father, those wide brown eyes with long curling lashes, he had his full lips and long slender limbs, he only had my button nose. He looked the same as his father as he slept, breathing quietly, nostrils flaring gently. Devon felt good to have become a father, I think he felt that somehow Marlo would have restored some of that lost feeling between us, but that was just it, we were fine only as a threesome. As far as he was concerned I was slowly pushing him out. He felt he didn't have a place in my life anymore.

'You'd rather work than spend my spare time with me,' he'd say.

'You could get a day job and give up this one,' I'd reply.

He'd offer his reasons why it would be beneficial to our relationship if my job was given the chop, reasons that usually implied that his job was superior in every respect including needs. We slowly slipped without realising it into our separate little worlds.

How he had changed. He wouldn't compromise, he wouldn't share, he wouldn't include me or involve me. His gains were his gains. He had tasted a nothingness and was determined not to squander the wholeness he now felt. My chest ached as my thoughts continued, my head throbbing with the memories of this final episode.

I was too busy to force myself into Devon's privacy and too weary to demand complete attention. My mouth was dry, I needed a drink of water but I couldn't move, my legs felt heavy like blocks of lead. One night he had gone to work as usual whilst I had put Marlo to bed and was soaking in the bath. I had reached for the warm bath sheet but had dragged his trousers off the adjacent peg instead. It had lain there on the bathroom carpet willing me to read it. I tried to force it back into the pocket it had fallen out of but I couldn't. I unfolded the coloured note paper, pink it was and cheap.

'Hi Dev. Thanks for a lovely time. Next time stay for breakfast...'

I dropped it into the bath. I felt sick, deep down in the pit of my stomach. I sat down on the toilet seat, the water dripping and forming neat patterns amongst the blue pile. Somehow I had always half expected it, but not now. I shouldn't have been going through his pockets anyway. I grabbed the floating piece of paper and tried to dry it on the damp towel. I folded it wet and purplish pink and pushed it deep inside Devon's trouser pocket. I calmly scrubbed the bath and dressed. I'd make a cup of tea and think about it properly. There was a drop of brandy left — I'd have that instead. I loved Devon, I wanted Devon. We could talk this through, we could sort it out. The neat handwriting had imprinted itself on my mind, 'Hi Dev. Next time stay for breakfast...' He had said that he preferred to be called Devon, he disliked abbreviations. If we talked we could sort it out. The brandy burned my throat and it felt good.

We had been kidding ourselves for months that we could go on the way we were. We didn't know each other anymore. We had drifted apart day by day, our relationship merely plodding with us. God I hate him. Why? Why did he have to do that? Why couldn't he have just gone? I took another fiery sip. My head was swimming with independence with neat brandy and neat handwriting. Perhaps it was my fault, I should have spent more time with him, I should have seen it coming. I had gone to bed and cried until my eyes were swollen. I hadn't slept a wink and as soon as it was light and he was home I confronted him. He denied nothing. It was my fault. He wanted out.

We had squeezed each other so tight. We had hugged and kissed and then gone to bed. We had over indulged our son one last weekend together. I remember begging him to stay, but we both knew he couldn't. He left.

I gulped. I was parched. Funny, but I didn't really hate him. At first I had blamed him for our parting, but in a way I was relieved. I hated him for his cowardly exit, then again I suppose it was his way of dealing with our weary situation. Most of all I was relieved it had finally ended. He came to see Marlo regularly which was a blessing because Marlo missed his doting dad. We were civil towards one another.

The rain had stopped rapping against the window. The branches did not swish or sway, the leaves did not rustle. The radio continued to play and I recognised the song. It was by Ken Boothe and the song we had danced to those years ago. This time my eyes pricked with tears and I saw the tall, broad shouldered frame. For a fleeting moment I wished Devon to be there with me. I held Marlo closely and rocked us both to sleep.

NAYABA AGHEDO

Bodyguard

Gedri drew on his cigarette and checked the clock once more. Four hours left. Next to him, Taiwo tossed restlessly. He looked over at her. She was beautiful. A rush of fear swept over him, and he squeezed her arm gently. He knew if caught in the crossfire, it could be him lying on the slab tomorrow, and not The Brother.

Almost twenty-two years to this day — his bosses had calculatingly dragged him out of Reverend King's bodyguard unit. No way was he gonna let it happen this time. Believing in The Brother, he knew he would die protecting him if he had to. Gedri got up — the tightness in his stomach almost unbearable by now. Going through to the cabinet he poured himself a neat whisky. Sure, he needed a clear head, but he needed to get a hold of his nerves first. He picked up the photograph on the side — his arms were around Taiwo and the girls, Jinike and Olunde. Whilst Imani, almost a man now at fifteen, stood proudly next to him. If he were to die what would become of them? Imani had college, and already bitterly argued against the conflict he felt between his Father's police profession and the struggle The Brother and all African-Americans were engaged in.

Maybe he should wake up his wife. Taiwo could always calm him down. Yeah, he'd question the Chief as to why security was so visible this time. Usually

The Brother spoke and guards were present, but reluctantly so, or merely protecting the hecklers. He'd tried to get through to The Brother himself and warn him; today he was going to die. Those in power would see to it — and all the security the Department would provide, wasn't gonna prevent the Department sniper reaching his target. That's how they worked. Bastards.

And he...big, top-ranking member of American law-enforcement was helpless.

He...proud African descendant and follower of The Brother, a part of the very establishment to kill him; aware hours before that he was gonna die. But, The Brother was not afraid to die, and probably knew that this rally maybe his last — knew before all of them, even before the gunman was chosen.

Gedri slumped into the chair by the window, and he cried. He cried for himself, for his predicament, for his Brother. Why was he weak in this hour of decision? Should he resign? Or should he go out with the unit today and try his best to keep The Brother alive?

Taiwo, awoken by her husband's absence from her side, entered the room and embraced him. Gedri felt like a child. His head fell to her breast, and he breathed in her deep, African musk.

'Woman love me' he wept, in the native tongue of his forefathers. She nodded, no words were needed. She understood.

And Gedri, relieved, knew then what to do.

LORETTA HARRIS

Parents and Grandparents

The girl walked slowly out of the small countryside primary school. At the gate, she could see her mother's red and white spotted head scarf. Immediately she felt a strong rush of love, but this was short lived for she remembered the cruel taunts she had received at school that day, taunts about how she was conceived from the devil because of her mother...She didn't want to think about it anymore, didn't want to believe, lies! Pure lies!

'Sarah, what time do you call this,' her mother furiously called. 'Have you been daydreaming again?'

Sarah looked around the playground. There was not a soul to be seen anywhere besides herself and her mother. She'd thought that the teacher had kept her behind for just a couple of minutes but it must have been longer...

'Well, I'm waiting for an answer,' her mother snapped.

Sarah sought in her mind for a lie, anything to keep from telling her mother the truth. For if her mother knew that the teacher had kept her behind to ask if she was having problems at home, why she had been acting quieter than usual that day, the whole truth would come out and then what.

'Sarah.'

'I was just helping Mrs. Bennett to wash out the paint brushes.'

'What! Until this time. Doesn't she think you've got a home to go? Blooming cheek. I've a good mind to give her a piece of my mind. In fact I think I will...'

'Please don't momma, it's not her fault. I asked if I could help and she said I could. She just forgot about the time, that's all.'

Sarah's mother looked down on her tenderly and her anger disappeared. She hated confrontations anyway.

'O.K. but next time I won't be so understanding.' She said grudgingly.

Sarah heaved a sigh of relief. That had been too close for comfort.

'Come on. Let's hurry home. I've made your favourite, shepherds pie, and it's just you and me tonight my girl. Your grandad's gone down to the pub to play darts.'

Sarah heaved another sigh of relief. She hated her grandad, especially now. She tried to look happy for her mother, but she wasn't happy. Not one bit.

Her heart ached, and she wished she could tell someone so the ache would stop. She had nearly told her teacher but she had chickened out at the last minute. Sarah knew that soon she would have to tell someone, anyone, not her mother though. For how could her mother ever love her again if she found out the truth. But hadn't the other children at school told her about her mother, that very same day? No, she didn't want to listen — simply to escape.

'What's the matter Sarah?'

Sarah looked up to see her mother looking down on her in a very concerned way.

'Nothing.' She lied quickly. 'It's just my head, it hurts a bit.'

'Well never mind, we're home now. You go and lie down and I'll bring you up something to take the pain away.'

Sarah made her way slowly to the room. Why was life so sad? Why did grown-ups act so strangely? Even more, why were they so secretive? These were just a few of the questions going through her mind as she changed out of her school clothes and neatly hung them up. Later, her mother did bring her something for the pain in her head...but nothing for the pain in her heart.

'Sarah, are you feeling any better?' her mother called upstairs.

'Yes momma.' She lied.

'Well then come down while your dinner's still hot.'

Sarah thumped noisily down the stairs, her footsteps echoing the way her heart felt — heavy. She had to ask her mother about what the other children had been teasing her about. Even if it meant causing a lot of pain she had to, just had to.

'Oh there you are, tuck in now while it's hot.'

Her mother chatted endlessly through the meal, about the bills and how that nosey Mrs. Jones next door, kept spying on them. But Sarah was in a world of her own, looking down at her barely touched food.

'Why Sarah. What's wrong dear? You've hardly touched your food and it's your favourite. You've got to eat something you know, or you'll never grow into a big strong girl!'

She smiled to herself remembering how she had sat at this very same table, she couldn't have been more than Sarah's age when her mother had said those very words to her. Funny how life recycled.

'DON'T WANT TO EAT. DON'T WANT TO GROW INTO A BIG STRONG GIRL!'

'Why Sarah, don't take on so. What's brought all this on then?'

Sarah stared back at her mother, large brown eyes shimmering with tears ready to be let forth, her small lips quivering.

'M-m-Momma' she stammered. 'Where's my real Daddy?'

She watched carefully as the strange look passed

over her mother's face. A look that had always haunted her whenever she asked her mother that same question.

'I-I told you before dear, he passed away soon after you were born.' She said much too quickly.

'Momma, at school today, some children in my class were teasing me, about me not having a father around. And then, one of the older girls told them to leave me alone, and she turned back to me and asked if I had understood all what they had been saying.I didn't answer her and she shrugged and mumbled something about me only being a seven year old kid, so I probably wouldn't understand anyway. But I did momma, I swear I did and now I want to know if what they're saying is true.'

She watched as her mother hurriedly got up and began clearing the table, muttering to herself about how the kids of today knew too much for their own good, and how in her day children were seen and not heard...

'Momma!'

The voice silenced her mother's tongue.

'Momma. Please tell me if what they're saying is true?'

There was pleading in her voice.

'I-I d-don't know what you are talking about, is what true?'

'Momma, will you please stop ignoring me and tell me if it's true...that grandad is really my father.'

There was silence for a second, no two, no three and then a strangled cry came from her mother's throat.

'I-I d-didn't w-want you t-to f-find out.' She burst out. 'I-I c-couldn't st-stop him.'

Then the story came out between muffled sobs and half finished sentences. Finally she made a single statement.

'Please can you forgive me?

She now looked at her daughter as if seeing her for the first time. Only it wasn't her daughter she was seeing, but an older, more sensitive girl. A girl who now walked up to her and put her arms around her, as if she now were the child and her daughter the adult.

'It's O.K. momma. I understand. For he has done the same to me lots of times.'

BIOGRAPHIES

Nayaba Aghedo
I have written for a number of years and now earn a living as a free-lance journalist and writer. I enjoy the powerful creativity writing inspires in me, and the debate the written word stirs in others. Presently I am writing a history book for children and am looking forward to having my own book of poetry published later this year. The power of the pen has often been used as a weapon of subjugation. I hope my small contribution will aid the process of liberation. In writing as in life laughter is as important as tears and vice versa in any circumstance.

Cindy Artiste
I am a Black American, resident in Britain since 1979. A playwright by profession, I was delighted when two of my poems appeared in the *Black and Priceless* anthology last year. Currently I am dividing my time between work on a novel *Disfigurations* and a play *The Potential Kid* which is sponsored by an Arts Council Writer's Bursary and questions the tyranny of I.Q. tests.

Jolina Black
I completed a two year youth and community course at Manchester Polytechnic. At present I am studying for a degree in Social Policy and Administration. I have attended a number of drama workshops and have performed in a play in Leeds called 'Roots in Boots'. In order for me to keep up with my two beautiful but hyperactive daughters, April and Amanda, I have taken up meditation. At weekends I enjoy visiting my very supportive mother. My poems are a reflection of my life.

Georgina Angela Blake

I am twenty nine years old. I went to school in Rugby and to college in Northampton where I studied a B.A. Honours in English and Social Studies. I moved to Manchester four years ago and at present I work as a teacher of English at a comprehensive school in Wythenshawe. I have been writing poetry since I was eight years old. My interests include reading, theatre and films.

Lorna Euphemia Griffiths

I started to write when I began to realize I had lived eighteen years of expected invisibility. The time had come to let people know I existed with needs, thoughts and feelings of my own. I forced the muzzle and the silent observations I had internalized as an obedient citizen I was ready to shout in their faces. These two pieces were written when I felt and shouted. I hope to shatter the ear pieces of the muzzlers who judged me a dumb robot.

Lorraine Griffiths

I'm not a *real* Jamaican. Let me explain. I was born in the island's capital — Kingston — in 1962 the year of our 'independence'. But, I've got a strong Lancashire accent which real Jamaicans find funny. Most of them have never heard of Bolton, either. Then again neither have the Londoners amongst whom I now work and live. An ignorant bunch who really have no excuse for claiming not to understand me. Still, I suppose I'll always be a displaced person — an African-Jamaican-English-Boltonian a long way from home.

Loretta Harris

I was born on 5th January 1970, the youngest of six children. At the age of five, I enjoyed telling stories, whilst my teacher wrote them down. This seemed the only time in lessons that I would really be happy, and probably that was what prompted me two years later, after I had written my first proper story, to vow to my parents that I would become a writer. I am now nineteen and still at college but still remain true to this statement, which I made twelve years ago.

Sua Huab

I was born in Wigan in 1969 of Somali/English parentage and lived there until I was eighteen. Living in an almost completely white area for this number of years made the creation of any kind of Black identity virtually impossible; and this is one of the many reasons I value writing so highly. I have been writing for about five years now and have been fortunate enough to have poetry published in *Perceptions of the Pen*, 'Moss Side Write' and *Black and Priceless*.

I am at present reading a degree in Social Policy and Sociology and eventually hope to work in equal opportunities in the North West.

Gloria Knowles

I was born in the West Midlands nearly twenty six years ago of Jamaican parentage.

I started writing in 1982 for churches and the 'Thought for the Day' radio slot a little later.

Since moving to Blackpool in 1987 I have displayed my work in various places and have read for Radio Lancashire whilst being a care assistant.

I give talks to different groups and based on this received a special 'Livewire' award for business enterprise in 1988.

I have had work produced in the Caribbean Times and a poetry anthology produced by Lit Fest.

Carlene Montoute

There was never a time when I didn't enjoy writing.

Even as a child I would play around with words, sometimes not knowing what they meant until I discovered the dictionary, then there was no holding me back.

For a period I was a member of 'Blackscribe' poetry performance group and was also involved with Frontline, Culture and Education in their production 'Struggle for Freedom'.

'Simmy', the first story in a collection of six gave me immense pleasure to write. I hope that this story appeals to you whatever your age and that you grow to love the character as much as I do.

Sally Neaser

I was born on Thursday 29th October '64 in a mother and baby home in North London. My mother who is from London's East End brought me up on her own.

I moved to Manchester on 2nd May '85 where I began to take writing seriously. I write about things I see, things I hear and the things I feel.

I never knew my natural father from Antigua West Indies until I was 21. Neither did I know about the West Indies which was expected of me because of my skin colour.

I have a two year old son who is Black. I have a Black brother and sister and two white sisters and brother. I am proud to call each of them my family

Pauline Omoboye

I was born in Manchester in 1958. I am a mother with four children who are a great inspiration to many of my poems. Writing poetry has been an enjoyable pastime for many years. Since attending the Black womens writing course organised by Cultureword I decided to take my work more seriously, I continued writing and began performing through Manchester's first Black womens' writing workshop 'Nailah'. I performed at the International Radical Black bookfair in 1988, and I am published in 'Moss Side Write', *Black and Priceless*, 'We Are Here' and 'Sistahs'.

Annette Reis

I was born in Stockport. My mother is of mixed race and my father is Nigerian.

I am a divorcée with five children and I have been interested in writing since I was a child. I have never before submitted any work to be considered for publication.

I have been a professional singer in the past and have recently begun to write songs and sing again.

I also dance with a contemporary dance group (amateur) and we raise money for charity with our performances.

I am a part-time teacher of English to speakers of other languages and also Adult Basic Education. I have a B.Ed. Degree which I gained as a mature student and a certificate in teaching E.S.O.L. (R.S.A.).

Kanta Walker

I wrote my first poem at the age of seven under a Shisham tree. Since then I have regularly written poetry or poetry has written ME.

In June 1959 I came to England on a scorching day holding a bunch of roses but it hasn't been all Sunshine and Roses!

I have spent most of my life working with Asian women as a community worker and have seen the proliferation of racism and race-related industry. The apparatus has rarely achieved anything for the women who are daily facing deportation, dole queues and violence — radical politics rarely reaches them.

My poetry is about people, places and situations I feel deeply about and need to say something. I like to hit back when I have had enough — it is the only way to stop my knuckles bleeding.

I am a painter so I like to visually create an image in words which I can later translate into a painting. Both the art forms link up to create multi-dimensional images for me.

About Commonword

Commonword is a non-profitmaking community publishing co-operative, producing books by writers in the North West, and supporting and developing their work. In this way Commonword brings new writing to a wide audience.

Over a period of ten years Commonword has published poetry, short stories and other forms of creative writing. *Talkers Through Dream Doors* is the fifth title to be published under the **Crocus** imprint. Forthcoming books include *Relative To Mc...*, a collection of short stories about families, and *No Earthly Reason?* a volume of poetry about the environment.

In general, Commonword seeks to encourage the creative writing and publishing of the diverse groups in society who have lacked, or been excluded from, the means of expression through the written word. Working class writers, black writers, women, and lesbians and gay men all too often fall into this category.

To give writers the opportunity to develop their work in an informal setting, Commonword offers a variety of writers' workshops, such as Womanswrite, the Monday Night Group, and Northern Gay Writers.

Cultureword which is a part of Commonword, and which acts as a focus for Asian and Afro-Caribbean writers, organises the Identity Writers' Workshop. Cultureword also co-ordinates 'Identity' magazine, and a writing competition for Black writers.

In addition to writers' workshops and publishing, Commonword offers a manuscript reading service to give constructive criticism, and can give information and advice to writers about facilities in their immediate locality. 'Writers Reign' magazine contains both information and new writing.

Commonword is supported by: the Association of Greater Manchester Authorities, North West Arts and Manchester Education Committee.

The Commonword/Cultureword offices are at Cheetwood House, 21 Newton Street, Piccadilly, Manchester. Our phone number is (061) 236 2773. We would like to hear from you.

If you've enjoyed reading Talkers Through Dream Doors, *why not try some of our other recent books?*

Now Then

This new collection of poetry and short stories looks at lifestyles, work and leisure from 1945 to the present day. In 'Home For Whitsun' Elsie Maskell recalls the spectacle and excitement of the Salford Whit Walks. Ron Redshaw relives his comical boyhood adventures down by the river in 'Going Back On The Irwell'. Change and continuity is looked at humorously by Maureen Tottoh in 'For Judy', as she compares the fashions of then and now. For other writers it is their experiences of the world of work that remain the most vivid, as Nell Harwood depicts in 'It's My Life Isn't It?' These are just a small selection from the writing contained in *Now Then* which powerfully evokes the flavour of a crucial period in recent history.

"This book gives a vivid account of a host of changes...sometimes funny, sometimes cynical, the authors give a down-to-earth view of Northern working-class life." (Oldham Evening Chronicle)
£3.50   108 pages   ISBN 0 946745 55 2

She Says

She Says is a new collection from five women writers celebrating the vitality and variety of women's poetry today. Pat Amick writes movingly and skilfully about her feelings for her father, of childhood joys and of the bitter-sweet nature of romance. Cathy Bolton's work deals with relationships, and the way in which they are constantly cut across by questions of power, the past and sexuality. Anne Paley's poetry has a searching and reflective quality, whilst describing situations that affect many women. Sheila Parry uses powerful images, culled from folklore, myths and fairytales, in her work, whilst Cath Staincliffe expresses her thoughts about love, motherhood and politics in a way that is always challenging and original.

"This collection of poems is rich and varied in form and content and always thought provoking. Read it." (7 Days)

£2.95   96 pages   ISBN 0 946745 50 1

Black and Priceless

Black and Priceless is an exciting collection of poetry and short stories by Black writers. The skill of Asian women's writing is illustrated by the work of Deepa Banerjee and Debjani Chatterjee, whilst in Peter Kalu's 'The Adventures of Maud Mellington', we have a hilarious detective story with a difference. The poetry of John Lyons tells with passion and energy of the experience of living with racism in this country, whilst Sally Neaser writes movingly of her feelings about motherhood. This selection of twenty-one writers includes those who are fast becoming familiar names, alongside others for whom this book represents their debut in print. A highly readable and diverse collection, *Black and Priceless* reflects the power of Black ink!

"All the pieces in this work have a positive strength, and the direct use of language is raw and powerful... **Black and Priceless** *is a timely eruption of a new and expressive black consciousness."* (City Life)

£3.50   200 pages   ISBN 0 946745 45 5

Holding Out: Short Stories by Women

Holding Out contains a compelling and challenging selection of writing. With both humour and pathos, this collection vividly portrays women's lives. The stories in the book take the reader from a still birth in 1930's Lancashire in 'The Confinement', through to a disturbing tale of child sex abuse in 1980's Britain in 'Daddy's Toy'. 'A Pair of Jeans' describes how what may appear to be a simple item of clothing can wreak havoc in the life of an Asian family, whilst 'Nothing Happened' is an affectionately wry look at life on the dole. These are just a small selection from this collection of twenty-one stories, which demonstrates both the strength, and the variety, of contemporary women's writing.

"This impressive collection of new work is sincere and honest, and it's enjoyable because the women featured cope with their lives with strength, courage and most of all, humour." (City Life)

£3.50   150 pages   ISBN 0 946745 30 7

Poetic Licence

Poetic Licence is an exuberant and bubbling brew of poetry from a diversity of poets living and working in Greater Manchester. Their work celebrates the many pleasures of poetry from the serious and intense, to the playful and humorous.

This book contains work from some exciting new poets. There's writing from the Black Writers' Workshop, and Northern Gay Writers, as well as from 'Chances' — a group of disabled and able-bodied writers, and performance poetry from Stand and Deliver. Peter Street writes movingly of old age and disability, whilst Anne Paley looks at life in the '80s as a woman, there's poetry in patwa from Patrick Elly, and short witty pieces from Gary Boswell.

"There are many different emotions and moods to be found within these pages and, read in its entirety, the whole volume is disarmingly powerful...Excellent value for money." (City Life)

£2.50   208 pages   ISBN 0 946745 40 4

Autobiography

Australian Journal: Alf Ironmonger　　　　　60p
In 1946, off the coast of South Australia, two young
shipmates decide to jump ashore. This is their tale...
ISBN 0 946745 01 3　　　　　　　　64 pages

Dobroyed: Leslie Wilson　　　　　　　　£1.20
The unique inside story of one person's experience of
a year spent in an approved school.
ISBN 0 950599 74 3　　　　　　　142 pages

Fiction

Marshall's Big Score: John Gowling　　　　£1.20
A book about a love affair, played out against the
backdrop of the gay scene in London, Liverpool and
Manchester.
ISBN 0 946745 03 X　　　　　　　76 pages

Turning Points: Northern Gay Writers　　　£2.95
This collection of short stories and poetry explores
moments of crisis — turning points — in the lives of
a variety of characters, with various different
conclusions...
ISBN 0 946745 20 X　　　　　　　120 pages

Poetry

Between Mondays: The Monday Night Group £2.50
This collection of poetry is the latest book from
Commonword's Monday Night Group. It brings
together some promising new writers with plenty to
say about life in the city, sexuality, Catholicism and
many other subjects.
ISBN 0 946745 35 8　　　　　　　104 pages

Liberation Soldier: Joe Smythe £2.50
Employing a variety of styles, Joe explores the discontents and disturbances of the times, from inner city riots to apartheid in South Africa.
ISBN 0 946745 25 0 84 pages

Hermit Crab: Di Williams 30p
Using the imagery of the sea and the seashore, these poems tell of a daughter's journey towards independence.
ISBN 0 946745 15 3 28 pages

Consider Only This: Sarah Ward 30p
A selection of poems which captures the atmosphere of moorland, cotton mills and small town life.
ISBN 0 946745 04 8 28 pages

Diary of A Divorce: Wendy Whitfield £1.00
Wendy Whitfield reflects on the breakdown of her marriage in a series of poems and cartoons.
ISBN 0 9505997 7 8 28 pages

Forthcoming Titles

No Earthly Reason? £3.50
A poetry anthology looking at the environment and how it affects us all — from the world on the doorstep to global issues!
ISBN 0 946745 65 X
Publication date: 10 October 1989

Relative to me... £3.95
Families — love 'em or hate 'em, this book of short stories will both move and delight you.
ISBN 0 946745 70 6
Publication date: 14 February 1990

ORDER FORM

TITLE	QUANTITY	PRICE	AMOUNT
Now Then		£3.50	
She Says		£2.95	
Black and Priceless		£3.50	
Holding Out		£3.50	
Poetic Licence		£2.50	
Between Mondays		£2.50	
Liberation Soldier		£2.50	
Turning Points		£2.95	
Hermit Crab		30p	
Consider Only This		30p	
Marshall's Big Score		£1.20	
Dobroyed		£1.20	
Australian Journal		60p	
Diary of A Divorce		£1.00	
No Earthly Reason?		£3.50	
Relative to me...		£3.95	
		TOTAL	

Please send a cheque or postal order, made payable to Commonword Ltd, covering the purchase price plus 25p per book postage and packing.

NAME: ....

ADDRESS: ....

....

.... Postcode ....

Please return to: Commonword, Cheetwood House, 21 Newton Street, Manchester M1 1FZ.